Start a Food Business
For Fun and Profit
in a Single Weekend

By Andy LaPointe

Website: www.StartAFoodBusiness.com

Published by Lapte Enterprises, Inc.

7053 M-88 South, Bellaire, MI 1-231-533-8788

Visit www.StartAFoodBusiness.com to learn about the complete food business training course.

Other Books and Course by Andy LaPointe

- Five Day Weekend – How to Leverage Your Time and Your Income to Achieve the Ultimate Lifestyle www.FiveDayWeekend.com

- Festival Profits – How to Make Money at Fairs and Festivals www.FestivalProfits.com

- Your Internet Consultant – How Maximize Your Social Media and Internet Marketing ROI for Small Business Owners and Executive www.YourInternetConsultant.com

Legal Disclaimer:

Table of Contents

Legal Disclaimer: 3

Copyright Information: ....**Error! Bookmark not defined.**

Resource Section: ....**Error! Bookmark not defined.**

My Story... 8

   One of my first jobs... 8

The First Step in Starting your Food Business 13

Who Will Make Your Product? 15

   You Produce Your Own Product in Your Own Kitchen.. 15

   Using a "Shared Kitchen" to Produce your Product 24

   Hire a Co-packer to Produce Your Recipe 25

      Tips on Finding the Right Co-Packer... 26

   Private Label Another Company's Recipes 27

   Use a Combination of All of the Above Methods 29

   Setting Up Your Food Production Facility 30

Operating Your Food Business 31

   Setting Up Your Legal Structure.. 31

   Determine the Legal Structure of your Business.. 31

      Sole Proprietorship:.. 31

      General Partnership: 33

      Limited Partnership: 34

      C Corporation:... 35

Subchapter S Corporation: 36

Limited Liability Corporation: 36

Writing a Business Plan 37

Good Manufacturing Process 39

Getting Permits 39

Business Costs 40

Estimating Food Costs 40

Estimating Labor Costs 40

Estimating Transportation Costs 41

Estimating Insurance Costs 41

Additional Food Business Expenses 42

Sales Tax ID and UPC codes 43

Determining the Right Prices for Your Products 43

Cost-Based Pricing Method 44

Percent Food Cost Pricing Method 45

Target Return Pricing Method 46

Value-Based Pricing Method 46

Retail and Distributor Price Sheets 46

Getting Your Recipes Ready for Mass Production 47

Standardizing your Recipes 47

Food Weight and Measures 49

General Information 50

Liquid Measurements 55

Solid Measurements 56

Product Labeling..57

Product Distribution, Marketing and Branding Strategies 58

Product Label Design 58

Food Competitions.. 60

Product Testimonials.. 62

Selecting the Right Domain Name 62

Attending Trade Shows.. 63

Attending Street Fairs and Festivals... 64

Working with Distributors and Retailers 64

Creating an Online Presence 65

Additional Requests to Get Your Food Business Set Up: 65

• Resource Section: .... **Error! Bookmark not defined.**

My Story...

I grew up in an entrepreneurial and foodie family. Since I was 8 years old I remember picking the green beans from the garden in the backyard, helping my mom cook in the kitchen and taste testing the dozens of Christmas cookies my dad baked every holiday season. For me, food was always a part of life. Usually food accompanied a time when family and friends enjoyed quality time and made lasting memories. From family reunions, birthday parties, funerals and graduations, food always played a role in the milestones of my life. Even in school I was in the kitchen. Here is a photo of me in the kitchen from my elementary school year book. (Photo below is not highest quality)

One of my first jobs...

One of the first jobs I had was working in one of my uncle's pizzerias. My uncle was a franchisee of a large pizza company in Michigan. He owned a number of pizza places and even had a commissary to supply all the raw ingredients for his pizza stores.

At the age of 12, I started working with my cousins in their pizza stores. I remember sweeping the floors, washing the dishes and keeping the windows clean. As I grew older, I continued to work with my cousins in a number of their stores as well as their commissary. I remember delivering pizzas, making the pizza dough, grinding the chunks of mozzarella cheese, and making deliveries of the raw materials to the pizza stores at 2:00 AM in the morning. I worked from time I was 12 years old until I went to college and as I look back at all of the great memories, it was one of the best times of my youth.

Living through that early experience is maybe why I always enjoyed spending time in the kitchen. I fully understood what it took to make a great tasting two item pizza. To the novice Friday night pizza lover, the pizza was simply a quick-n-easy way to have a good meal, but to me it meant much more. It meant hours of learning how to put together just the right mixture of pizza sauce, cheese and pepperoni to provide the perfect balance of flavor.

Not too much one ingredient, but just enough of everything to make a great balanced taste. I still remember standing in front of a hot pizza oven hours during a busy Friday night and painstakingly removing the fully cooked pizza pie from the pizza oven and placing it into a box for customers. To me it was almost paradise.

Maybe that is why almost 20 years later I am back in the food business. A business not only offering great food, like my uncles pizzerias, but a business that teaches about the natural health benefits of simple everyday food. Not only does my business offer gourmet fruit-based products, but it also offers an entire line of super fruit supplements.

Since we launched our business over 7 years ago we have won 14 national awards including 7 Scovie Awards. We own several food-related trademarks and have been awarded a patent by the United States Patent and Trademark Office. That's me holding a few of our salsa and one of the national awards we won at America's Best National Food Competition.

In addition, our products are distributed locally, regionally, nationally and internationally. We have product testimonials from movie stars, world-class athletes and everyday folks. We have also received a "Special Tribute" from the State of Michigan that is signed by the governor of Michigan congratulating us on the national awards we won.

We have also had fun with our business. For example, our logo was entered into Entrepreneur Magazine's Ugliest Logo in America contest and we won. To many people that would be to embarrassing the win the ugliest logo contest, but by being the winner of the contest we received a free logo redesign worth over $500 and national media coverage.

The image we wanted to project with our first logo was a healthy and all-natural look. We wanted a logo that included water splashing on the shore, a bright sun and a green meadow. If it sounds pretty complicated for a logo, it is. But as you can see, we completely missed the look we were hoping for. When you look at our first logo it looks like a blue bird sitting in a nest with an orange blob of something above it.

Here is our logo before we won the Entrepreneur competition:

And here is our new redesigned logo after we won the competition:

Our redesigned logo is a significant improvement from the first logo. It's crisp and to the point and provides the exact image we are seeking for our Traverse Bay Farms brand. I will provide with additional insight on logo design in the marketing and branding strategies section later in the book. But as you can see, having a food business can be fun, even if you are voted as having one of the ugliest logos in the United States.

The only reason I share this with you is not to impress you but to impress upon you how far your food products and recipes can take you. Your recipes can take you as far as you want to go. Your recipes can give you and your family the financial success you desire. It can also give you the personal satisfaction of knowing that something you created is giving others pleasure and enjoyment in life.

All it takes is a plan, hard work and ability to adapt your business to the ever changing opportunities of the marketplace. But what makes you unique is that you have that special recipe. Maybe it's a recipe your grandmother handed down to you or maybe it is something you created yourself. You may be in possession of the recipe so special that you know if you can get people to taste it they will want it. That is why I wrote this book and created this complete step-by-step course.

This book is a complete roadmap to bring your recipe from concept to creation and finally to market. In the following pages, you'll find checklists, questionnaires, resource sections and more to help you start your very own food business for fun and profit. In addition, as a bonus, in the resource section I include a list of recipes that you can use to help you find additional recipes to add to your line or use to create your very own signature recipe.

The First Step in Starting your Food Business

Depending on your location, you may or may not need to use a commercially licensed kitchen to produce your recipe. Although, if your state has passed any law called a "Cottage Food" law you may be able to make your recipe in your own home kitchen.

You see, in my State of Michigan, the legislature recently passed a Cottage Food law. The recently passed Cottage Food law allows individuals to manufacture and store certain types of foods in an unlicensed kitchen.

Foods that can be manufactured in a home kitchen in the State of Michigan are non-potentially hazardous foods that do not require time and/or temperature control for safety. These types of food include: breads, jams and jellies that can be stored at room temperature, non-potentially hazardous dry bulk mixes that are repackaged, cotton candy, nuts, pretzels and more.

However, the distribution channels for the foods produced under the recently enacted Cottage Food law are extremely limited. According to the law, Cottage Foods cannot be sold over the Internet, by mail order, to a restaurant or for use in a restaurant or to wholesalers, brokers or distributor who would in turn resell the Cottage Foods. However, the law does state Cottage Foods can be sold directly to the consumer at farm stands, farmers' markets, roadside stands and other venues including street fairs and festivals. You may want to check with your local and state government to see if a similar Cottage Food law exists.

The purpose of this book is not to teach you how to create great tasting recipes or share culinary secrets. The mission of this material is to provide you with a plan to take your recipe to market. It doesn't matter if you only have an idea for a recipe or already have produced a few cases of your product. The information contained in this book will show you step by step what you need to do to bring your product to market. In addition to traditional methods of marketing your product, you'll also learn innovative ways to market your product online. You'll learn marketing strategies that never existed five years ago, but are vital to ensure your success today.

I firmly believe it is much easier to bring a food product to market today than it was ten year ago. The reason is you have so many more ways you can market your product and make multiple streams of income.

In addition to being a guide, this course has a number of videos and manuals. The reason I created this format is because I want you to have all of the tools you will need to get your product to market fast. In addition, you'll also learn about all of ways we can help you get your recipe into the hands of store buyers, website owners and the end consumer.

Remember, I am making the assumption you already have an idea for a recipe, a recipe itself or a finished product. The first step in starting your food business is deciding who is going to make your recipe. Will you personally be making your recipe or will you hire someone to do it for you.

In the next section, you'll learn about the different ways of producing your recipes. Believe it or not, some of the most well known and respected brands in the specialty food industry are not actually produced by brand themselves. So let's turn our attention to the different ways for getting your recipe produced.

Who Will Make Your Product?

You have several choices of production capability when you are building your food company. One method is not better than another when building your business. You simply need to start where you stand and use the information in this book to help you make the best decisions for you, your family and your business. You may find you will start your business following one production strategy, and as your business grows, you'll switch to another production strategy.

Below are examples of each:

- You produce the product in your own home kitchen
- You use a "shared kitchen" to produce your product
- You hire a co-packer to produce your recipe for you in their kitchen
- You private label another company's recipes
- You use a hybrid of all of the above
- Setting up your own food production facility to produce your recipes

You Produce Your Own Product in Your Own Kitchen

For some of the readers, due to local laws, producing a commercial recipe in your home kitchen is allowed. However, for other readers this may not be permitted. Even if you are not currently permitted to produce your recipe in your own kitchen, you still need to understand this option. This type of home-based business operation is usually referred to as "Cottage Food" or "Artisan Food". Usually cottage kitchens are unlicensed kitchens and have restrictions on the types of recipes produced, the production capacity, maximum sales volumes, how the products is distributed and more.

The State of Michigan were I live, has enacted a cottage food law for food entrepreneurs. Although the following example references the State of Michigan

Cottage Food requirements, they do vary from state to state. However, I want to include an overview of the State of Michigan Cottage Food Law requirements to give you a starting point with the type of requirements and restrictions that are involved in operating a cottage kitchen. The following references the State of Michigan Cottage Food law only. **This information is not all inclusive and not legal or health advice**. Consult your health department and the Michigan Department of Agriculture & Rural Development for comprehensive Cottage Food Law regulations, requirements and restrictions.

Here is a non-comprehensive, brief overview of the State of Michigan Cottage Food law:

What are Cottage Foods? Cottage foods are referred to as the specific types of foods that you manufacture in your single family domestic residence kitchen.

What does a single family residence include? This is where you live. This includes your own the home or if you are renting. Thus, an apartment, condominium, etc. are all considered a single family domestic residence. However, this definition does not include group homes or communal settings including sororities or fraternities.

What types of Cottage Foods can I produce in my home? Non-potentially hazardous foods that do not require time and/or temperature control for safety. Brief example of some of the types of Cottage Foods that are allowed to be produced in my home?

Breads and cakes (wedding, birthday, etc.), jams and jellies (that can be stored at room temperature), cookies, dry herbs, dry baking mixes, dry soup mixes, popcorn, cotton candy, chocolate-covered food (pretzels, strawberries, pineapples, Rice Krispies treats, marshmellows), roasted coffee bean.

Brief example of some of the types of Cottage Foods **ARE NOT ALLOWED** to be produced in my home?

Fish and fish products, meat and meat products, canned products (including salsa, apple butter, pickles), Hummus, all beverages (apple cider, etc) salad dressings, pet foods, barbeque sauce, products made from fresh cut tomatoes or cut melons

Are pet treats included under the Cottage Food Law?
The Cottage Food Law applies to human grade food only.

How do I sell my Cottage Foods? The law allows you to sell your Cottage Foods directly to the consumer at direct-to-consumer venues. This includes farmers' markets, farm stands, roadside stands and similar venues. The important this is you are selling your finished product directly to the consumer. Cottage foods cannot be sold in the following venues:

- To a retailer for resell
- To a restaurant for use
- To a restaurant for resell
- To distributors or brokers for resell
- By mail order or over the internet

Why does the Cottage Food Law stop me from selling to a restaurant or grocery store? Since the Cottage Kitchen is unlicensed and not inspected, the food handling practices are not inspected and evaluated by a food safety individual. This means, the handling practices of the kitchen are not inspected and reviewed so the final product is not considered an approved source for use in a restaurant or resale in a grocery store.

Do I have to put a label on my Cottage Food? Yes, the law requires you to label your Cottage Foods. Here is the basic information that must be included on your label:

- Name and physical address (not PO Box) of the operation.

- Name of the product.

- The ingredients of the product, in descending order of predominance by weight. In addition, if you are using a prepared item in your recipe, you must list the sub ingredients on the label as well. For example: Enriched flour is not acceptable, is should say Enriched flour (Wheat flour, niacin, reduced iron, thiamine, mononitrate, riboflavin and folic acid)

- Net weight or net volume (must also include the metric equivalent)

- Allergen labeling as specified in federal labeling requirements.

- The following statement: "MADE IN A HOME KITCHEN THAT HAS NOT BEEN INSPECTED BY THE MICHIGAN DEPARTMENT OF AGRICULTURE AND RURAL DEVELOPMENT" must be on the label. This statement must be at least the equivalent of 11-point font (approximately 1/8" tall). In addition, the color of this font must provide a clear contrast to the background.

MADE IN A HOME KITCHEN THAT HAS NOT BEEN INSPECTED BY THE MICHIGAN DEPARTMENT OF AGRICULTURE AND RURAL DEVELOPMENT

Chocolate Chip Cookie

John Smith
879 MyTown Lane
Maple City, MI 54342

Ingredients: List all of the ingredients here

Net Wt. 16 oz (454g)

What does "Allergen labeling as specified in federal labeling requirements mean?" This means you must specifically identify if any of your ingredients that are made from specific food groups. These food groups include: milk, eggs, wheat, peanuts, soybeans, fish (including shellfish, crab, lobster or shrimp) and tree nuts (such as almonds, pecans or walnuts). In addition, if you have an ingredient made with a wheat based product, you have two options:

1. List the allergen in the ingredient list. For example, a white bread: whole wheat flour, milk, sugar, water, salt and yeast. In this example, the statement 'whole wheat flour', meets the requirements of federal law.

2. Include an allergen statement ("Contains:") after the ingredient list. For example a white bread, with the following ingredients: whole wheat flour, water, sodium caseinate, salt and yeast. Contains wheat and milk.

- The "Contains" statement must reflect all the allergens found in the product. In this example, the sodium caseinate comes from milk.

Are there any special requirements for tree nuts labeling for allergens? Yes, if your Cottage Food has tree nuts as an ingredient you must identify which tree nut you are using. For example, if you made the following product:

- Nut Bread, an acceptable ingredient list would be: wheat flour, water, almonds, salt, yeast. The following would not be acceptable: flour, water, nuts, salt, yeast.

Are there any other limits I need to know about Cottage Foods? Yes, you are limited in the amount of money you can make selling Cottage Foods - which is $15,000 gross sales annually per household.

Can I make the Cottage Food products in an outbuilding on my property, like a shed or a barn? No, the law requires the Cottage Food products be made in your kitchen and stored in your single family domestic residence. Approved storage areas include the basement and attached garage of the home where the food is made.

Will I need to meet my local zoning or other laws? Yes, the Cottage Food exemption only exempts you from the requirements of licensing and routine inspection by the Michigan Department of Agriculture.

What oversight does the Michigan Department of Agriculture have over my Cottage Food operation? Cottage Food operations are considered to be food establishments, but will not have to meet most requirements outlined in the Michigan Food Law. In all cases, food offered to the public in Michigan must be safe and unadulterated, regardless of where it is produced. As a Cottage Food Operator, it is your responsibility to assure the food you make is safe. In the event a complaint is filed or a foodborne illness is linked to your food, the Michigan Department of Agriculture will investigate your operations as part of our responsibility under the Michigan Food Law. As part of that investigation, it may be necessary for the Michigan Department of Agriculture to enter and inspect your Cottage Food production and storage areas, view and copy records, and take photos during the course of a complaint investigation. The Michigan Department of Agriculture also has the right to seize product suspected of being adulterated, order corrections of label violations, or require you to discontinue making unapproved products.

Are there any additional requirements regarding my home on-site well or sewage system?

No, although annually testing your well for coliforms and nitrates is recommended. Contact your local health department for sampling containers and directions.

Does my equipment, stove and/or refrigerator need to be NSF (a food equipment evaluation group) approved? As a Cottage Food operator, you would not be required to meet NSF standards for your equipment used to manufacture the Cottage Food product.

Can I bake bread in a wood fired oven? Yes, as long as that oven is in your home kitchen.

Do I need to have a DBA for the Cottage Food law? A DBA (Doing Business As) may be a requirement of your county or local municipality;

When are Cottage Food products subject to sales tax? The Cottage Food amendments are to the Michigan Food Law. The amendments do require that the Cottage Food Operators meet all other provisions of law regarding businesses, including tax law. MDA recommends that you contact the Michigan Department of Treasury for further information on what food products are considered taxable.

The above cottage food law information was provided by courtesy of the State of Michigan. A special thank you to the State of Michigan

If you are in an area that allows Cottage Food production, make sure you fully understand any and all of the restrictions before you make your first batch. Contact your local health department to clarify any questions you may have.

The main benefit to producing your recipe in your home kitchen is the low cost to start up. To get started, you would simply need ingredients, jars, and a place in your home to make your recipe. Thus, your costs are minimal.

Although you may have the ability to operate your business out of your kitchen, you still need to get business insurance. You need business insurance to cover loss, recall of your product, etc. Make sure you meet with a competent business insurance broker to fully discuss your insurance needs prior to making your first batch of product.

Using a "Shared Kitchen" to Produce your Product

If your state doesn't offer a cottage food law or you don't want to produce your recipe in your own kitchen, the next step would be to use a shared kitchen.

A shared kitchen is just as the name implies. You share a commercial kitchen with other food entrepreneurs. A shared kitchen is a licensed facility where recipes not suitable for home kitchen production (potentially hazardous foods) are produced. A shared kitchen is the first step between a home kitchen and a fully licensed and large scale commercial kitchen. The greatest benefit of a shared kitchen arrangement is these facilities usually have state-of-art cook equipment that you are able to use for a very nominal fee.

Unlike home kitchens you have the ability for full production capability, distribution outlets and business development options usually not available to home kitchens. In addition, you'll have the ability to conduct public cooking demonstrations and meet other food entrepreneurs that you can share knowledge and experience.

Hire a Co-packer to Produce Your Recipe

A co-packer is a fully licensed kitchen that you can hire to produce your recipe to your specifications. A co-packer frees you up from the actual production of your recipe so you can focus on getting your recipe out into the world. You simply pay the co-packer a per jar fee plus any additional set-up fees and they will produce, box up and pallet your finished product. In essence, a good co-packer provides a complete turn-key experience.

Here is a brief overview of the advantages and disadvantages of working with a co-packer.

Advantage of working with a co-packer:

- Low start-up costs as compared to buying equipment and building a facility
- Knowledgeable co-packers can assist in product development, food safety testing, shelf-life studies, etc.
- Co-packer may have similar products, thus reducing production time and saving you money.
- Already familiar with Good Manufacturing Practices, Hazard Analysis and Critical Control Points (HACCP), regulatory certifications, etc.
- Co-packers have the ability to purchase and maintain inventory on raw materials, space to store your finished product and may even be able to provide fulfillment capability to your retailers and distributors.
- Provide assistance with label design, provide contact information for food brokers and more.

Disadvantage of working with a co-packer:

Working with a co-packer can also have its disadvantages. Here are some of areas you should be familiar with when working with a co-packer.

- You will need to disclose confidential information including your formulations, recipes, etc. Thus, when working with a co-packer you should consider having a non-disclosure form signed prior to disclosure of any confidential information.
- You give up all control of the production process and production schedule.
- The co-packer may already be producing a similar product to yours, thus creating a potential conflict of interest.
- If the co-packer gets into financial trouble, you need to know if their financial troubles can potentially have a lien placed against your finished products prior to delivery to you.

Tips on Finding the Right Co-Packer

Now that you have a better understanding of many of the advantages and potential pitfalls of working with a co-packer, let's turn our attention to finding and qualifying the right packer for your product.

Usually the large co-packers have more experience, better financial stability and more production capability than a start-up. However, they usually also require higher minimum production runs which can be an issue for a small start-up food company.

In addition, shipping costs are also a concern. For example, if your co-packer is in another state, shipping costs from their facility to your location can really add up. Thus, start your search for a co-packer near your current location. This not only reduces shipping costs, but will allow you to visit your co-packer in-person.

Finally, when interviewing co-packers ask for samples of finished product samples the co-packer has produced and references of current customers. Visit the resource section to view a brief list of co-packers kitchens by listed by state.

Private Label Another Company's Recipes

Private label (PL) is when a product is manufactured by one company so another company can put their brand name or label on the finished product. PL products are also known as private label branding, store brands, and private-label goods. For instance, the next time you are in the breakfast cereal aisle of your favorite grocery store read all of the names on the cereal boxes. You'll probably find several different types of cereal with the name of the grocery store on the outside of the box. The finished product you are seeing on the shelf is usually manufactured by another company but the grocery store has "private labeled" the product.

In addition to offering many of the same benefits of a co-packer, here are some of the additional benefits a PL kitchen can provide:

- Add Products Fast - Since you are not making the product you don't have to worry about source the raw material or retooling your production line. You simply find a company with a recipe you like and then you can add the new product to your current line usually within weeks.
- Start with an idea – There are a number of PL companies that offer a number of products you can build a company around in almost any niche you desire.
- Start with only one recipe - If you only have one recipe, you can go out and find complimentary products and offer a complete line of products.
- My company offers private label of the products we offering including the Traverse Bay Farms salsa's, dried fruit and more.

The main benefit of private labeling recipes is it allows you to focus exclusively on growing your company and building your brand. While the greatest disadvantage is the recipes aren't your own. You are simply placing your label on another company's recipe.

Use a Combination of All of the Above Methods

As your business grows, you may find your business is using a combination of all of the production methods we have covered so far. For example, when you get started you may be producing your own recipe in your home kitchen or in a shared kitchen. You could then add complimentary products from a PL kitchen, thus allowing you to expand your product line without any equipment investment or hiring additional employees. As you gain more experience and create additional recipes you may decide to hire a co-packer to produce these additional recipes that you created. As you can see, the only limitation in the food business is your imagination. If you get overwhelmed with orders or recipe ideas you can always hire a co-packer, PL or a combination of these to keep your business growing and moving forward.

Setting Up Your Food Production Facility

This section is designed to provide an overview of what is needed if you decide to set up your own food production facility. The very first step in setting up your food production facility is to check with the local zoning ordinances to determine if you can actually run your business in your desired location. Local zoning regulates the type of business that can be operated in certain areas of your area city. If you have any questions regarding zoning, contact the zoning department of the local governmental office.

You shouldn't make any plans to build, remodel or rent a suitable facility until you fully understand the zoning law for your area. Remember, unless you are exempt from inspection, as determined by the local, regional or State law, don't start production in your facility until you are inspected by the local health department.

When selecting a facility to rent or purchase make sure that you have adequate delivery capabilities. This includes the ability for delivery trucks and semi trucks to easily access your location. For example, you may find an ideal building in a busy downtown location and sign the lease for the business only to realize the alley behind the building is not large enough to allow semi-trucks to deliver to the facility.

In addition to planning the delivery capabilities of your facility, you need to consider disposal, too. Since a food processing business generates waste you need to determine how you are going to dispose of it. Contact your local health department to help determine disposal procedure for your business.

Operating Your Food Business

Setting Up Your Legal Structure

In this section, we'll learn more about setting up the legal structure for your business and in the next section, we'll learn more steps to actually producing your recipe.

You see, you need to set up the proper business structure to protect yourself, your business and your recipe from any sort of liability issues regarding the structure of your business. In this section I am going to provide you with a brief overview of the different type of business structures.

Determine the Legal Structure of your Business

One of the first step's to starting a company is to decide on the type of business structure you will assume. The size of your business usually determines the type of legal structure. If you want your business structure to be relatively simply and you don't have partners you can consider structuring your business as a sole proprietorship. If you have a few people who will join in the venture consider a partnership structure. In this section you'll learn about the type of business structures.

Sole Proprietorship:

The sole proprietor business is an individual that owns and operates the business. In the sole proprietorship business, there is no legal separation between the business and individual. The individual enjoys 100% of the profits and is personally responsible for 100% of the debt and liabilities of the business. The person who wishes to operate a business under the sole proprietorship arrangement must file an Assumed Name also known as "Doing Business As" or a "DBA" in each county where the business is located. You'll need to contact the county clerk to learn more about filing a DBA.

Here are the advantages and disadvantages to forming a sole proprietorship:

Advantages	Disadvantages
Simple to start	Difficult to raise capital
Retain all of the profits	Unlimited Liability
You control all of the decisions	Inexperience in business ownership
Low cost start up	Inexperience in product marketing
Tax Advantages	Lack of ability to pass along to next generation

General Partnership:

A partnership is when two or more persons join together in the formation, operation and management of a business for a profit. General partnerships are relatively easy to start. With this type of business arrangement, all of the partners are liable for all debts of the business. All of the profits of the business are taxed as income to the partners based upon each partners percentage of ownership. Like a sole proprietorship, a partnership must file DBA with the county clerk's office where they do business.

Advantages	Disadvantages
Simple to start	Difficult to raise capital
Tax Advantages	Unlimited Liability for at least one partner
Able to benefit from the collective experience of the partners	Committee to make decisions
Partners to help in decision making process	Difficult in finding suitable partners
Tax Advantages	Partnership terminates when one partner leaves

Limited Partnership:

A limited partnership has two or more individuals. In a limited partner arrangement, there are two types of partners, a general partner and a limited partner. The general partner has the same rights as partner in the general partnership arrangement. The limited partner is not generally liable for the obligations of the business. The general partners may receive cash and other assets and also incur unlimited liability. Limited partners can only receive proportionate profit shares as indicated by the partnership agreement.

Advantages	Disadvantages
Simple to start the business	Partners are personally liable for obligations of
Low start up costs	Not available in all states
Tax Advantages	

C Corporation:

A corporation is a legal entity that has its own rights and liabilities separate from those forming the corporation. A corporation can own property, enter into legal contracts and do almost anything a "real" person can do. A corporation has a board of directors, shareholders and corporate officers. This type of business is subject to more government regulation than proprietorships or partnerships. In addition to having the advantages of limited liability to the shareholders, this type of structure makes the corporate earnings subject to double taxation. In order to form a corporation, "Articles of Incorporation" must be filed.

Advantages	Disadvantages
Simple to start	More regulations
Easier to raise capital	Additional record keeping
Transfer of ownership	Expensive to start
Large pool of expertise	Double taxation

Subchapter S Corporation:

An S Corp is a special section of the IRS code that offers special tax advantages including the ability for the profits to be taxed at the individual rate, rather than a corporate rate.

Advantages	Disadvantages
Avoid double taxation	Some restrictions
Losses offset owners income	Must operation on a calendar year for reporting

Limited Liability Corporation:

The Limited liability corporation can be treated as a partnership for income tax purposes and provides the limited liability of the corporation.

Advantages	Disadvantages
Limited Liability	Procedures vary from state to state
Tax advantages than corporation	Transfer of ownership may be more difficult
Lower start up than corporation	
More management flexibility than corporation	

In addition to speaking with an attorney and/or account to help answer your questions about the most appropriate type of business structure for you, here are several websites to do your own research, too.

- Legal Zoom.com
- IncorporateNow.com

Make sure to check out the resource page on our website for a more detailed listing of incorporating your business online. The resource link is in the resource section near the end of this book.

When dealing the accountants and attorneys, I have found it is best to work with someone you feel more comfortable dealing with assuming they are competent. Over the years, we have worked with several accountants and attorneys all across the United States. The reason we have worked with different professionals is each is able to offer unique competence. For example, our main FDA attorney is based in Washington DC. He is one of the nation's foremost FDA attorneys. He is very expensive but is worth every dime. If we have a question regarding any FDA requirements, we simply pick up the phone and he is able to answer our question.

Our trademark and patent attorney is based in Chicago. He has extensive expertise regarding trademark and patent applications. Our CPA and general council attorney is located in our area of Northern Michigan. Both have offered insight into the growth our business. The benefit of modern technology is you can work with almost anyone in any location on the globe. As you get started, it may be best to start locally so you can have face-to-face meetings to get everything set up and when you need specialized expertise you can always search the Internet for the best fit for your business. If you can't find it locally you can go national.

Writing a Business Plan

When starting your own food business you'll need to write a complete business plan. Since writing a business plan is so vital to your success and is a very detailed topic in its own right, I have included a complete module on how to write a successful business plan in the resource section of the website. Thus, I will not go into any further detail of how to write a business plan in this book.

Good Manufacturing Process

When producing and selling food for human consumption, your business must conform with Good Manufacturing Practices (GMPs). GMPs were designed by the federal government to ensure that foods are manufactured, processed, and handled in a safe and sanitary manner. To operate your business, you must meet the conditions as set forth in the GMPs. GMP procedures usually include the following areas:

- Building
- Production equipment
- Maintenance of facility, grounds and equipment
- Sanitation
- Processes and controls
- Personnel

Contact your local health department for a complete overview for your specific area.

Getting Permits

Check of the local health department to determine the type of permits required to operate your business. Here is a non inclusive list of the type of health permits. Depending on your location and business, the names and exact requirements for each permit may change.

- Retail Food Store Permit, covers grocery stores
- Food Service Establishment Permit, covers restaurants and any food service businesses, including catering businesses
- Food Processing Permit, covers food processing businesses

- Food Warehousing Permit, covers food distribution and food wholesalers

Business Costs

Your business will have both fixed and variable expenses. Fixed expenses usually do not change, such as rent. In addition to budgeting for fixed costs, you will need to budget for start up costs. These usually include one-time costs including equipment, office furniture, license fees, etc.

Variable costs are expenses that change from month to month. Examples include utility bills, ingredient costs, supplies, transportation, advertising, etc.

Estimating Food Costs

In the food business, you need to estimate the cost of ingredients on a per unit or per dozen basis. Make a list of the ingredients needed for your recipe and then contact several food distributors to compare prices. When first starting your business, you may be purchasing your ingredient list from local retail grocery stores and wholesale outlets.

However, as your business grows, you'll want to stream line your ingredient purchases and have them delivered to you rather than buying from the local grocery store.

Estimating Labor Costs

In the beginning, you may decide to work for free, but your employees won't. When creating your budget, always include a labor cost for yourself and your employees. Even if you aren't pulling a salary, it is good business practice to have realistic expenses in place.

For example, when estimating labor cost divide the profit by the hours spent to produce the final product. For example, if it takes 25 hours of labor to produce a $100 profit, the labor cost is $4 per hour. You also need to determine what your time is worth and add in the cost of your personal labor. You may decide to pay yourself $5 per hour or $25. This amount is up to you. Consult your accountant to help determine hourly wage estimates.

Remember, labor cost is more than simply preparation time. Employee time is required for product transportation, purchasing, and recordkeeping. Although family member may work for free, you should also include a fair and reasonable wage for their efforts too.

Estimating Transportation Costs

Consider the following questions. Will you deliver your products? If so, include gasoline and other automobile costs as an expense. Is a unique vehicle necessary? Will you need equipment to keep foods at recommended temperatures while in transit?

Some foods have to be kept cold while being delivered. Let's use the example of ice cream. Ice cream needs to be kept frozen at all times or the high quality of the product is lost. Consequently, if you plan to sell ice cream, you must purchase, rent, or lease a refrigerated truck to transport it. To determine which is suitable for your company you have to ask another question: Can you recover a prorated price of the delivery automobile, which includes fuel and maintenance?

Estimating Insurance Costs

Insurance is vital to your business. It can help keep your business secure against losses from fire, illness, ingredient recall and injury. Talk with a business insurance agent to understand the options available.

Here is an non-inclusive list of insurance options you may want to consider for your business:

- **Product Liability Coverage** to protect your business if your product causes injury
- **Product Recall Insurance** to help cover the cost to recall a product from the market
- **Business Income Insurance** to help cover loss of income if you need to suspend operations if your business suffers income loss caused by fire, etc.
- **Auto Insurance** is to cover a car used to support the business in any way
- **Worker's Compensation** if you have employees
- **Disability Income Protection**, a form of health insurance in case you become disabled
- **Business Life Insurance** to provide funds upon the death of key employees. This may help to offset any financial setback that may occur with the death of a key employee.

Additional Food Business Expenses

Ask your accountant to provide you with a list of applicable expenses for your business. Here is a brief list of expenses to help get your started:

- Customers who do not pay
- Accounting fees
- Legal fees
- Production leftovers, product pilferage, returns, and "mistakes"
- Food wrap, napkins, and condiments

- Online advertising
- Offline promotion

Sales Tax ID and UPC codes

In addition to permits, you'll need a federal tax ID number. A 9-digit number is assigned by the IRS and used to track business taxes. You can contact your accountant to assist you with getting a tax ID number or contact the IRS at www.IRS.gov.

You can also get a federal tax ID number from the following website: www.federalnumber.net

A UPC code is allows your product to be scanned and purchased at the grocery store registers. Thus, a UPC bar code required if you want to sell your product in retail grocery stores. The obtain a code, explore the following website: http://www.gs1us.org/

Determining the Right Prices for Your Products

How much should you charge? The answer to this question is vital to your success. Do you want to be the highest price product (higher profit per item but usually lower volume) or the lowest priced product (lower margins but usually higher volume) in your niche? Both has its advantages and disadvantages. If you decide to sell your product above the market, you'll need to offer additional benefits to justify the increased price. For example, if the selling price of your ice cream is 25% above your competitors you could provide a free ice cream recipe book with each purchase.

By having a higher margin, you'll usually have the increased profits to offer additional add-ons with your products. On the other hand, if you are the lowest priced product in your niche, you are competing on price alone and usually another competitor will offer an even lower price grab market share. You need to be very careful if you decide to compete on price alone.

When deciding on the price of your products, consider what similar products are selling for in your niche and talk with others to help determine your final selling price. Below are a few pricing strategies to help get you started:

Cost-Based Pricing Method

This method determines the selling pricing by using ingredient cost, expenses and labor

For example, your fixed expenses are $100 per month and you work 2 days per week or 64 hours per month and you're the ingredient cost is $0.80 per each jar of jelly; and you can make 100 jars in an hour. How much should the price be for each jar?

1. Calculate the total hours working to produce the actual product. Ten hours of the 64 are spent in delivering your product, selling the product, bookkeeping and buying ingredients, thus these activities are not included in the production costs. Thus, the total hours to produce your product are 54 (64 − 10 = 54).

2. Calculate the total expenses per hour. Divide your monthly fixed expenses by the total production hours worked in 1 month ($100 ÷ 54 hours = $1.85 fixed expenses per hour to produce your final product).

3. Calculate the ingredient cost per hour. Take the total cost of your ingredients ($0.80 per jar) and multiply it by the number of jars you can produce in one hour ($0.80 x 100 = $25). Make sure to add the cost of the label to your calculations.

4. Calculate your labor cost. Say you want to pay yourself $15 per hour.

5. Add all of the totals together:

Fixed expenses	$1.85
Ingredients	$80.00
Labor	$15.00

Total per hour cost $96.85

6. Take the total cost per hour and divide it by the number of jars of jelly you can produce per hour ($41.85 ÷ 100 = $.96). This means you have to charge at least $.96 per jar to cover your costs.

Percent Food Cost Pricing Method

This method is used mostly by restaurants. The percent food cost method is based on the theory that total food cost makes up about 40 percent of the final price. Thus to set a price for menu, multiply the food cost by 2½ (40 x 2½ = 100 percent).

For example, let's say the cost to produce a deli sandwich is $1.75. Take this total cost and multiply it by 2.5. In this example the final menu price should be $4.50 (rounded up). The percent food cost is ideal for food products that require large labor costs such as restaurants. The reason is restaurants have a number of people working in the business including cooks, servers, waitresses, etc.

This method can also be used if you plan on opening a catering business. However, in the catering niche, you would multiple your cost by three and not 2 ½. The reason for this increased multiple is you have additional expenses in the catering niche including additional transportation costs, equipment to keep the food warm and more when compared to a restaurant.

Target Return Pricing Method

This method is used to set your price to achieve a return on investment or ROI. For example, so you invest $10,000 into your company and estimated sales volume for the first year is 5,000 units. You want to recoup your investment in the first year so you would need to make $10,000 profit on your total sales. So you would need a profit of $2 per unit.

Value-Based Pricing Method

This method is creating a price based upon the value your product creates for the customer. This is the most profitable form of pricing. Let's say you sell a loaf of bread that cost you $1.75 to produce and you believe you can sell your product for $5 per loaf. However, the competition is selling similar loaves of bread for $3. You can add additional value to your product by offering a one-hour free cooking class at your kitchen for each loaf of bread purchased. You offer an additional value to the customer for the increased price point.

Retail and Distributor Price Sheets

Once you have your product produced and ready for the marketplace, you may decide in addition to selling direct to the consumer you want to sell your product to food distributors and retail stores. If you do sell your products through these additional channels you need to create retail and distributor price sheets. These sheets including price points, minimum orders, time needed to fill orders, etc. I have included examples of prices sheets later in this book.

Getting Your Recipes Ready for Mass Production

The key to getting your recipes for mass, either in your home kitchen or your commercial kitchen is to standardize your recipes. This process allows you to keep your costs steady and the ensure all of the final batches are uniform.

Standardizing your Recipes

Taking a small-serving recipe and increasing batch production is as simple as multiply the ingredients by the final production number you want to meet. For example, if you have a recipe that produces 10 serving and you want to make 100 servings you simply multiply the ingredients by 10.

In addition, make sure you keep track of any changes to your recipes. Even the smallest change to a recipe can have a big impact on the final product. Keepk track of everything you do regarding your recipes. Remember, it is your recipes that will make or break your business so keep your recipes in a safe and secure place. A home or office safe usually is adequate for recipe safety when you first get started.

In addition to keeping your recipes safe you also need to keep track of the following information too:

- Complete description of the product
- Quantity produced by each batch
- Serving size of the final product in weight, volume or number of pieces
- Equipment used to produce the finished product (pans, cooper kettle, etc.)
- Is the recipe cooked in glass or medal pans
- Order of ingredients
- Brand name of ingredients
- Where the ingredients are purchased

- Complete step-by-step instructions for preparation and ingredient combination, cooking time and temperature, etc.
- Create a manufacturing flow chart (MFC)
    - A MFC shows the steps necessary for your recipe to be produced. This provides an excellent overview of the recipe flow.

Food Weight and Measures

The purpose of weights and measures is to assist manufacturers in determining the metric equivalent declarations (e.g., gram (g) and milliliter (mL) measures) of the common household measures that are declared on food labels. When FDA performs nutrient analyses to determine the accuracy of nutrition labeling, assessment of compliance is based on these metric quantities.

The Nutrition Labeling and Education Act of 1990 added section 403(q) to the Federal Food, Drug, and Cosmetic Act (21 U.S.C. 343(q)). This section specifies, in part, that the *serving size* is "an amount customarily consumed ... expressed in a common household measure that is appropriate to the food," or "if the use of the food is not typically expressed in a serving size, the common household unit of measure that expresses the serving size of the food" should be used. For example, for a product such as pancake mix that is an ingredient of a food, if 1/4 cup of pancake mix is required to make the customarily consumed amount of pancakes, the serving size of this pancake mix would be expressed as 1/4 cup of mix.

Serving sizes are determined from the reference amounts established in 21 CFR 101.12(b) and the procedures described in 21 CFR 101.9(b)(2) and must be expressed in both common household measures and equivalent metric quantities (21 CFR 101.9(b)(7)). As stated in 21 CFR 101.9(b)(5) the term "common household measure" or "common household unit" means cup, tablespoon (tbsp), teaspoon (tsp), piece, slice, fraction (e.g., 1/4 pizza), ounce (oz), fluid ounce (fl oz), or other common household equipment used to package food products (e.g., jar, tray).

For specific details of the final rules that apply to serving sizes, refer to the following sections of the Code of Federal Regulations (CFR):

21 CFR 101.9(b)   **Nutrition labeling of food; definition of serving sizes**

21 CFR 101.9(b)(6)   **Single-serving containers**

21 CFR 101.9(b)(8)   **Number of servings per container**

21 CFR 101.12(b)   **Reference amounts customarily consumed per eating occasion**

General Information

1. Representative samples of a food should be selected using standard sampling techniques from various lots (Ref. 21 CFR 101.9 (g)(2)). For mixtures (e.g., solids in solids, such as brownies with nuts; solids in liquids, such as soup with vegetables) the sample selected should contain a representative amount of the incorporated solids.

2. Good quality laboratory equipment (e.g., graduated cylinders, balances, etc.) should be used to measure or weigh the food. Equipment should be calibrated in accordance with good laboratory practices and/or manufacturer's specifications.

3. Standard analytical practices should be used for accurately determining product weights and volumes. Significant digits should be retained in order to minimize

rounding errors in reporting final values.

4. Each set of measurements should be determined by the same trained operator using the same methodology (i.e., the same equipment, procedures, and techniques) under the same conditions. For variable products (e.g., small pastas, snacks) another set of measurements should be determined by a second individual.

5. All measurements should be replicated a sufficient number of times to ensure that the average of the measurements is representative of the product.

6. Foods and containers should be at appropriate and compatible temperatures for volume determinations. Foods stored at room temperature should be measured at 20°C, refrigerated foods should be measured at 4°C, and frozen foods should be measured at the frozen temperature.

7. The quality of the food product should be maintained throughout. Moisture gains or losses should be minimized. Fragile products should be handled carefully to minimize product breakdown. For example, flake breakfast cereals should be carefully transferred to volumetric containers and should not be sifted, stirred, or packed. Measurements should be made prior to excessive handling or shipping.

8. The food volume measured should be at least 10 times the reference amount for the category in order to minimize measuring errors. (For example, dividing the weight of a cup of a product by 16 and 48 provides the tablespoon and teaspoon weights, respectively.)

9. For purposes of nutrition labeling, 1 cup means 240 mL, 1 tablespoon means 15 mL, 1 teaspoon means 5 mL, 1 fluid ounce means 30 mL, and 1 ounce means 28 g (21 CFR 101.9(b)(5)(viii)).

10. As defined in 21 CFR 101.9(b)(5)(i), the household measures of cups, tablespoons, or teaspoons should be used whenever possible. Fluid ounces may be used for beverages. These measures should be expressed as follows:

Cups: **1/4, or 1/3-cup increments**

Tablespoons: **Whole numbers of tablespoons for quantities < 1/4 cup but ≥ 2 tbsp**

1, 1 1/3, 1 1/2, 1 2/3 tbsp for quantities < 2 tbsp but ≥ 1

Teaspoons: **Whole numbers of teaspoons for quantities < 1 tbsp but ≥ 1 tsp**

1/4-tsp increments for quantities < 1 tsp

If cups, tablespoons, or teaspoons are not applicable, units such as piece, slice, tray, jar, and fractions should be used (21 CFR 101.9(b)(5)(ii)). The fractional slice of a food that most closely approximates the reference amount should be expressed as follows (21 CFR 101.9(b)(2)(ii):

Fractions: 1/2, 1/3, 1/4, 1/5, or 1/6, and smaller fractions that can be generated by further divisions by 2 or 3 (such as 1/8, 1/9, 1/10, 1/12, 1/15, 1/16, etc.).

If other units are not applicable, ounces may be used and must be accompanied by an appropriate visual unit of measure, for example, 1 oz (28 g/about 1 inch slice of cheese) (21 CFR 101.9(b)(5)(iii)).

11. When the serving size is exactly half way between two values, it should be rounded to the higher value (21 CFR 101.9(b)(5)(ix)), for example, 2.5 tbsp is rounded to 3 tbsp.

12. Grams and milliliters should be rounded to the nearest whole number except for quantities that are less than 5 g or 5 mL. Gram and milliliter quantities between 2 and 5 should be rounded to the nearest 0.5 g or 0.5 mL. Gram and milliliter quantities less than 2 should be expressed in 0.1 g (or 0.1 mL) increments (21 CFR 101.9(b)(7)).

13. The provisions in 21 CFR 101.9(b)(7) exempt single-serving containers from listing metric equivalents except when nutrition information is on a drained weight basis in accordance with 21 CFR 101.9(h)(9). If companies voluntarily list metric equivalents for single-serving containers, the value must agree with the

net quantity of contents expression.

14. FDA is unaware of any need to make changes in the procedures for determining metric equivalents of household measures due to the effects of variations in altitude. The agency will consider the need for altitude corrections should data become available.

Liquid Measurements

1. Liquids may be measured in volumetric glassware or graduated cylinders. The level should be read at the lowest part of the meniscus and care should be taken to avoid parallax error. For clear liquids, a shade or dark material behind the meniscus may improve observation.

2. The volume being measured should be within 25 percent of the total capacity of the glassware selected. Select the smallest container that will hold the intended volume.

3. Techniques for determining the volumes of viscous liquids (e.g., syrups, molasses), fluid-type solids (e.g., applesauce, hot breakfast cereals), and spoonable thick or gelatinous solid-type liquids (e.g., gelatins, mayonnaise) include direct fill and volume displacement:

   a. **Direct fill** - Direct fill involves carefully transferring the product to avoid incorporating air bubbles, allowing time for settling (viscous liquids are higher in the center when first poured), and, if necessary, leveling with a straight edge or by extrusion. For example, for a hot breakfast cereal product, a density cup of known weight and volume may be used to determine the volume to weight relationship: the cereal is transferred to the measuring container, the sliding disk is moved into position leaving a small gap, the excess cereal escapes through the opening and is wiped away, and the weight of the known volume of cereal can be determined by difference.

   b. **Volume displacement** - Volume displacement involves adding a second material to fill the air space above the product. For example, a measured amount of water can be added to completely fill the air space above the mayonnaise in a mayonnaise jar. The volume of mayonnaise can be determined as the difference between the volume of the jar and the volume of water added. The material selected should not mix with the product being measured.

Solid Measurements

1. Fine particulate solids (for example, sugars, batter mixes, flours) may be leveled using a knife or other straight-edge after transfer to an appropriate volumetric measure (e.g., a cup measure would be appropriate for determination of tablespoons or teaspoons).

2. Medium particulate solids (i.e., nuts, flakes, pastas) should have the particle volume above the fill line approximately equal to the free air space found between particles immediately below the fill line.

3. For products where the packing liquid is not normally consumed (for example, olives, pickles, tuna fish, etc.), products should be drained for 2 minutes on a No. 8 sieve before weighing or measuring. AOAC procedures for canned vegetables and fish products are described in sections 968.30 and 937.07, respectively, of *Official Methods of Analysis* (Reference 1).

4. Products should be measured in the form in which they are packaged and sold (see 6 above). Some frozen products (e.g., frozen blocks of vegetables, frozen juice concentrates) cannot be transferred to volumetric containers in the frozen state. This type of product may need to be broken apart and/or defrosted slightly in order to fit into the measuring container. If necessary, cover and thaw the

product minimally, transfer to measuring container, and return the product to its frozen state for measurement.

5. Techniques for determining the volumes of bulk solids (e.g., bulk cheeses) and irregularly-shaped solids (e.g., ice cream novelties) include direct measurement and volume displacement:

   a. Direct measurement - Direct measurement involves creating a representative piece with regular dimensions. For example, the dimensions of a one ounce cube of cheese can be directly measured with a ruler.

   b. Volume displacement - Volume displacement involves immersing the irregularly-shaped object in a known volume of another material and measuring the amount of material displaced. For example, an ice cream bar can be dipped briefly into a vat of cold liquid. The volume of the displaced liquid can be determined directly or by difference. The amount of displaced liquid is a measure of the volume of the irregularly-shaped ice cream bar.

Product Labeling

Your label can make or break your product, especially if you are selling your product to distributors and retail stores. Your label represents your brand and creates your company image.

Here are a few items that need to be included on your product label:

- Name and complete address of the packer, manufacturer or distributor
- Net amount of the food in the package in both English and metric
- Font size for specific information on the label
- Common name of the food

- Descending list of the ingredients in the food
- Any allergens in the product (check with your local health department to get list of the major allergens that must be listed.)
- Nutritional information and nutritional facts. (check with your local health department)

After you have completed your label, contact your local health department and ask for a complimentary review of your final food label. They will usually provide this review at zero or a very nominal cost.

Product Distribution, Marketing and Branding Strategies

Product distribution, marketing and branding is vital to your success. No matter how good of a product you have, if the world doesn't know it exists your business will not succeed. Let's now turn our attention to getting the word out about your products to the world.

In this section I am going to address several different areas including distributing your products through distributors and retailers, creating marketing and branding strategies and selling your products online.

However, before you can market your product to the public you need a good label design. You have already learned what must go on your label from a legal standpoint, but now let's turn our attention to the actual label design aspect.

Product Label Design

An attractive label will not only make your product jump from the shelf into a customer's basket, but it will also increase your online sales. In addition many distributors and retailers require attractive labels for a product to even be considered for distribution.

While a good label design is in the eye of the designer, here are a few ideas to help you get started in designing your label.

- Good use of graphics

- Bright colors

- Show the customer what is in the bottle, bag or jar by using food specific images

- Simple, non-complex layouts and design

Here is an example of our Fruit Advantage line of super fruit products.

As you can see, the use of bright colors, food specific images and simplicity it really makes the product jump from the page. If you were walking through an aisle of dietary supplements, you would immediately know what our products were. You would know the Fruit Advantage Joint Formula is a cherry-based supplement, while the Fruit Advantage Brain Support is made with Wild Blueberries.

There are a number of online resources to finding good label designers for nominal costs. I have included several sources for designerd in the resource section of our website.

Food Competitions

Food competitions are an excellent way to get the word out about your recipes. Even if you only have one recipe, make sure you enter food competitions. Winning in a food competition is not only really cool, but it adds a lot of prestige to your company. We have gotten a lot of new distributors, wholesalers and stores carrying our products simply because of the awards we have won. Winning awards adds a lot of credibility to your products.

One of the best things about food competitions is you can enter as many and as often as you want. If you don't win in a given year, you can keep entering until you win.

You can either enter national food awards or get started locally, it really doesn't matter because once you win you can advertise your recipe as award winning and you get to place a bunch of really cool stickers on your products. As I mentioned, my company has won 14 national awards and here is an example of our salsa labels. As you can see, we 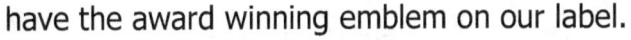 have the award winning emblem on our label.

Depending on your product, here is list of some of the national food competitions you can enter your products into:

- Scovie Awards
- America's Best National Food Competition
- Worldwide Mustard Competition

We have many more in the resource section of our website.

www.StartAFoodBusiness.com

Product Testimonials

Product testimonials are social proof that your recipe is a good product. Getting testimonials for your products help to increase sales and your prestige. So how do you go about getting testimonials for your products? Here are several ways you can go about getting testimonials for your products:

- Ask you current customers
- Ask the manager of the store that carries your product
- Send your products to local newscasters, radio personalities and editors and ask them for a testimonials
- Place a form on your website asking for testimonials

Selecting the Right Domain Name

When selecting a company name make sure the domain name for your company is also available. For example if your company is Green Creek Salsa Company, check to see if the domain name www.greencreeksalsa.com is available .

Picking the right company name and/or URL is vital to your success. Make sure they represent the image you want your customers to have of your website. Also, ask several people to review your name and URL to ensure there is not any potential for any sort misunderstanding of your name or URL.

Attending Trade Shows

Attending trade shows is an excellent way to get distributors and retails to begin carrying your products. Over the years we have attended countless trade shows both in the gourmet food industry for our award winning salsas and in the dietary supplement industry for our Fruit Advantage super fruit supplements.

You can attend regional or national shows. The regional shows usually draw attendees, distributors and retailers from specific areas, while the national shows draw across the entire nation. It has been our experience that local regional shows have been more profitable for us. Not only do they cost less to rent a space, usually $500 for a regional show compared to $3,500 for a national show, but we usually pick up more business since we are personally talking with the store owners and the owners of the food distribution companies. While at the national shows, it is usually the regional salespeople you meet and they usually don't have the ability to make the decision to bring your product in for distribution.

In addition, travel expense to attend a regional show are usually 50% less than a national show because you can usually drive to the show and do not have to worry about the extra cost of airfare.

Here are some of the shows to help get you started:

- Natural Product Expo - dietary supplements, health and wellness products, etc.
- Fancy Food Show – gourmet foods, grocery items, etc.

We have many more listing in the resource section of our website.

Attending Street Fairs and Festivals

Participating in local fairs and festivals is an excellent way to not only support your local community, but to generate immediate sales and cash for your business. Best of all, some street fairs and festivals only cost $10 - $15 to be a vendor and depending on what you are selling, you can make $500 to $1000 per day. That's a pretty good return on your investment.

We teach this strategy to all of our students as one of the best ways to grow your food business fast, but unless you know what to do, you'll simply be wasting your time and your money.

On average, my company attends 3 – 5 street fairs and festivals a month during summer festival season. Not only does this generate immediate cash flow, it allows us to receive immediate feedback on our products.

We have a complete module on selling at street fairs and festivals in the resource section of our website.

Working with Distributors and Retailers

Once you have your product produced and ready for the marketplace, you may decide to offer to sell your product to stores and through distributors. If you do sell your products through these channels you need to create retail and distributor price points. Getting this right the first time is vital to your long term success. If you don't get this right the first time, it is very difficult to change your price once you get your product in distribution with wholesalers, distributors and retails. The first step in working within these distribution channels is to create retail and distributor sales sheets and price sheets.

These sheets include product description, price points, minimum orders, time needed to fill orders, etc. We provide our distributor and wholesale partners a supply of these flyers so they can give them directly to the retail store owner and managers.

Here is a listing of some of the larger distributors:

http://www.unfi.com

http://www.treeoflife.com

http://www.gardenspotdist.com

We also have additional distributors in the resource section of our website.

When working with retailers one of the best things you can offer to do is product demonstrations. Product demos will not only help to increase sales, it shows the retailer you are serious about promoting your product and they will be more willing to place your product in store flyers, etc.

Creating an Online Presence

I have included several modules and over 8 hours of training videos to help you create a website and market your product online. View the resource section of our website for more information.

Additional Requests to Get Your Food Business Set Up:

Here is a brief list of office related material to help you get your business up and running fast. I have included a complete listing of companies for each bullet point in the resource section of our website:

- Business cards

- PO Box
- Toll-free telephone number
- Business checking account
- Graphic (label) designer
- Website designer
- An account with Stamps.com
- A UPS shipper account with UPS.com
- SKU numbers for your products
- High-gloss, digital label printer
- Merchant card to accept credit cards online and at street fairs

Resource Section:

Call Andy at 231-498-2401 so he can email you a complete downloadable resource manual that contains links to low-cost printers, graphic designers and more.